SPANISH DRAWINGS

THIS VOLUME, EDITED BY
Tana de Gámez Losada

IS ONE OF THE HYPERION DRAWING
SERIES AND WAS FIRST PUBLISHED
IN NINETEEN HUNDRED AND
FORTY NINE BY THE HYPERION
PRESS. THE BOOK AND JACKET WAS
DESIGNED BY DANIEL STONE.

SPANISH DRAWINGS
XV-XIX CENTURIES

by

JOSE GOMEZ SICRE

THE HYPERION PRESS
New York   Paris   London

Foto facsimiles by Giraudon, Anderson, W. F. Mansell, Alinari and The Hispanic Society of America.
Ancient maps from the New York Public Library.

PRINTED IN THE UNITED STATES
by
THE POLYGRAPHIC COMPANY OF AMERICA, INC.

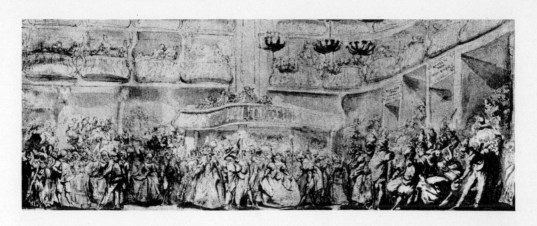

LUIS PARET Y ALCAZAR   Masked Ball in the Teatro Real at Madrid (detail)
British Museum, London

Few indeed are the drawings left to us by Spanish masters. Reasons for such limitations may be found in the underestimation of drawing as a medium of expression which the Spanish painters shared alike. Perhaps we may still find a better explanation in the very core of the Spanish spirit, in the lusty realism of the painting of Spain, alien to such profound intellectual executions as drawings. We find justification in the fact that few and unimportant are the drawings of Velázquez. After all, his passion for the plastic medium itself prompted him to plunge to work armed with brush and oil alone, which he brandished with incredible power. Yet, we must pause and wonder; were his masterpieces conceived without a structural inception on black and white? What mysterious cause has deprived us of the preliminary staff where Velázquez inevitably had to annote the origin of such wondrous counterpoint as "Las Meninas"? Apart from the clay figures with which el Greco studied the movements of his tortured subjects, what animated blueprint is left from the celestial explosion that is "The Burial of Count Orgaz"? In recognizing that these master ventured into projects of such magnitude without monocrome inceptions, we must admit we are dealing with unparalleled genius. Their dimensions take still greater proportions precisely because of the Spanish craft for impromptu and improvisation. When Spanish painting reaches its zenith, after merging the Gothic and Romantic influences into its very own Iberian entity, we find it a strong impressionistic painting. From here on the master seeks truth through life, essentially because of the sheer sensuous pleasure he finds in the pictorial matter itself. But in regard to contents Spanish painting is the painting of man, be it mystic or sceptic, a man close to earth, nevertheless. Marked by human failing he seeks God on earth, in his surroundings. Thus we find that the classic idealism of Italy in the XVI century had little bearing upon the art of Spain, which acquired something only from its dying phase, the Baroque, the vivid era of flowing life and bursting passions. To these aspects we must add the Spaniard's striving impatience to attain immortality. To perpetuate himself on canvas he would not adhere to the dictates of other cultures or cannons of idealization, as was tried by the Italians of the Renaissance. Nor would he stop to labor on exterior accidents in order to find inner profoundities, as customarily attained by the Flemish with minute detail. Reality for the Spanish painter was more a problem of emotion than description. This impression, whether turbulent or peaceful could not be arrived at through intellectual hesitation and evolution. On the contrary, one would harbor it in a vehement impetus that rested upon accents, sensations, on the quest for truth in man himself. A school of painting based on such principles would necessarily be short on intellectual exercises, for wisdom, in this case, was to leave the emotion find its own truth. Thus is the individualism and therefore the realism of the plastic art of Spain, which left no abundant legacy of drawings.

Yet, in the brief summary of Spanish drawings available, we can see the passing of time, the history, styles and influences which contributed to forge its own national art. We have in the X century evidence of the Islamic culture, especially in the illustrations of sacred books. In the XI and XIII centuries we have proof of the Romantic era, when the Catalonian painters maintained close contact with those of Siena, the great retreat of Byzantine art. In the XV century new blood is injected in the art of Spain: the minute realism of the Flemish, which was linked by the Spaniards with the Romanic sediment. This gave birth to an art which tried to reconcile the simplicity of one and the intensity of the other. The result was the first step towards a national art. Unified by the alliance of Castile and Aragón, Spain can boast of its first characteristic painter, Bartolomé Bermejo, towards the end of the XV century. The Flemish influence remains, but a certain independence has been added; realism searches for naturalism. Another school attempts to reconcile various antagonistic standards, Valencia, through Juan de Juanes. Here we find a tenuous inclination for the classic Romanticism of Raphael. And so the splendor of the Renaissance transcended to the Iberian peninsula. Castile continued to labor under nordic influences. Yet, one of its most distinguished painters, Pedro Berruguete, is known to have worked in Italy just then.

When Philip II initiates the construction of El Escorial towards the end of the XVI century, many European artists turn their eyes to Spain, coveting the fame and immortality that would inevitably result from collaborating in decorating an edifice of such magnitude. A protegé of the monarch was Juan Fernandez Navarrete el Mudo, who was influenced by his devotion to Titian and painted with the opulence he saw in the Venetian masters favored by Spanish royalty since Charles the V. It was here that Domenico Theotocopulos appeared in Spain. Called el Greco because of his Cretan origin, this fervent painter, disciple of Tintoretto and Titian swiftly became a thorough Spaniard. He was given opportunity to win royal acclaim with a small painting, but soon lost the favor of the court with "St. Maurice and the Theban

Legions". Perhaps his treatment of the subject did not conform with the established Spaniard reverence for religious paintings. It may also be that his unorthodox style was too advanced for conventional royal taste. El Greco took refuge in Toledo, decorating convents and churches and coming in contact with the pious devotion of his adopted land. This led him to create the most vehement painting of the Counter-Reform. From Toledo, without leaving one specific school, El Greco defined forever the depth of Spanish soul, tracing the way for the most brilliant period in the painting of Spain.

The XVII century is called the Golden Era of Spanish painting. Suddenly all tendencies and influences concord in one unity, bringing Spanish art to the radiance of maturity, creating a realism so starkly pure that it surpassed all other directions of the Baroque era. Early in the century, Francisco Ribalta, and later, his disciple Jusepe de Ribera, still found inspiration in the Italian source, in the romanism of Caravaggio. The method, transcribed by the Spanish mind, acquired the great emotional intensity that made Spanish painting the most peculiar of that century. Seville produces notable creators as Francisco Herrera the Elder, of vigorous execution; Francisco de Zurbarán, representative of the world of lights and shadows imposed in Spain by Ribera. In Zurbarán the dramatism of Ribera takes greater austerity. The Spanish soul appears behind the Italian influence to offer fruits of rich con-texture. Bartolomé Esteban Murillo, another Sevillian of high rank

in the painting of his time, is perhaps the most popular of Spanish painters. But his work in general presents such light and frivolous aspects
that he is only the favorite of the uninitiated. He seeks in his madonnas
the sentimental expression which he firmly believes to derive from
Raphael and Guido Reni. His work lacks strength and order in structural design. His drawings present the same weakness of expression
evident in his paintings.

Another native of Seville, Juan Valdés de Leal is a personal in-
tepreter of the tortures and martyrdom of the flesh. The energetic trac-
ings of his drawings are a magnificent example of Baroque art at its best.
Alonso Cano, also an Andalusian, has left us an illustrious production of
drawings. He showed great regard for sculpturing values in the
medium of drawing. His monocromes are surpassed in quantity only
by Goya. His landsman, Antonio del Castillo Saavedra, is another
creator who shows talent and inclination to produce effective contrasts
of lights and shadows in drawings, which in any case surpass the merit
of his paintings.

In 1606 the Spanish court settled in Madrid. The favorite of the
royal house was Diego de Silva y Velázquez, another native of Seville.
The favor he rated above his contemporaries is more than rightly justi-
fied. He became the most important painter of his time. His work
excludes the use of light in search of drama, of color for sheer flattery,
of melodramatic gestures and other resources used more or less success-

fully by the Baroque painters. His art dwells in the firmest reality. One can say that Velázquez was the first to liberate painting from the tyranny of the theme. The portrait to him is a plastic problem and not a narrative imposition. His few drawings lack the greatest characteristic of his work: the luminous color and the graceful brush stroke, learned from the Venetians through el Greco and later by a trip to Italy and finally placed by himself upon the most inaccessible summit in his century. With Velázquez Spanish painting reached the culmination of realism. The XVII century ended for Spain and for the art of Europe, but this Sevillian painter of the Castilian court of Philip IV inaugurated Spanish modern painting. After him, right in the very palace of his serene triumphs, his son in law, Juan Bautista Martínez del Mazo and Juan Carreño de Miranda tried with sincere dignity to perpetuate his executions. But they fell in the dangers of repetition and mannerism. It was then the task of a master of the following century, Francisco de Goya y Lucientes, to transmit to humanity the heritage of Velázquez, bringing it is a living element to our very days.

At the time of Goya's birth Spanish painting suffers from exhaustion. The few talents of the day return to foreign sources like Rubens, Tiepolo and Mengs in order to continue the Baroque tradition. Goya himself is influenced by Tiepolo at first. But what in his master becomes a race for the grandiose, in Goya turns to subtle irony, to sheer grace and freedom. Goya too became court painter at the royal palace. In search of the great secret of the color of light he dug deeply in tapping different resources. Just as varied were his themes, ranging from portraits to typical scenes and situations of his day; bullfights, political libel, social scandal, nightmares, carnal yearnings and human tortures, he recorded in the most naked and poetic realism. Worthy successor of Velázquez, Goya is the greatest artist of his epoch for the masterpieces he created, for what his work anticipated to future generations.

His production of drawings is voluminous. We learn that the illustrious Aragonese travelled drawing book in hand, picking up, like a modern reporter, the most vivid events of his journeys. Not only did he reproduce the incidents that struck his fancy, but giving it significance and meaning he frequently labelled such drawings with the most ironic reflections. It is the Spanish soul laughing at pain and death since the days of Ribera, Zurbarán and Valdés Leal. With the same ease that Goya records in frantic accusation the tortures and injustices that choke Spain on the return of Ferdinand the VII, he captures the Duchess of Alba with marvelous elegance and rhythm, during their escapade of 1796 to San Lúcar de Barrameda. In the frivolous, the sensuous, the horrible or the political debate, Goya overflows with passion, with that ardor that prompted André Malraux to say: "he is the greatest interpreter of the anguish known to the Occidental world". At his death in 1828, European art is at the turning point of the battle between the order and discipline of classicism, and

D R A W I N G S

the kingdom of emotion and the return to nature which the romantics uphold. Goya shall be disputed by both sides alike in the generations to come. And that is because Goya, like the other great masters of his country, has found in man and nature, in the emotion of form itself the wise affinity sought by painting, that is: the essence of the plastic through the most passionate themes. After Goya, Spain returns to an absurd stagnation. The romantics and the impressionists, the realists and the expressionists of Europe steal the teachings of the great Aragonese at every corner. Since then, Spain has not contributed to history a great creator, until the ripening of our own century brings us the powerful personality of Pablo Ruíz Picasso.

FRANCISCO PACHECO

National Library, Madrid

Portrait of a Poet

JOSE ANTOLINEZ 1639-1676

Born in Seville but attributed to the school of Madrid, where he studied with Rizi. His works are remarkable for color and tonality and probably never surpassed by any of his contemporaries. He died in his prime, victim of a malignant fever and suffering from a most unhappy disposition.

FRANCISCO BAYEU Y SUBIAS 1734-1795

Born in Saragossa and a pupil of Jose Luzan, who was later Goya's first teacher. He was influenced by Mengs and was appointed director of the Academy of San Fernando as court painter to Charles IV. Sometime before 1771 he was a teacher of Goya's whose early decorations he supervised.

RAMON BAYEU Y SUBIAS 1746-1793

Brother of Francisco. He studied in the Academy of San Fernando and won a prize in a competition for which Goya also entered. He was engaged by Mengs to paint tapestry cartoons and worked with Goya in the decorations of the Saragossa Cathedral.

ALONSO BERRUGUETE c.1486-1561

Son of Pedro, who probably was also his first teacher. Born at Paredes de las Navas and died in Toledo. Both a painter and a sculptor, Alonso Berrugete is best known for his works executed in sculpture.

JOSE CAMARON Y BORONAT 1730-1803

Director of the San Carlos Academy in Valencia, where he lived and died.

ALONSO CANO 1601-1667

Architect, sculptor and painter, born in Granada, a versatile craftsman, who in spite of his ability never has been considered a great talent. He was an intimate friend of Velazquez. He is known to have had a passionate disposition and was accused of the murder of his wife. The quality of his sculptures surpasses by far that of his paintings.

ANTONIO CARNICERO 1748-1814

Painter, engraver and etcher born in Salamanca. Studied in Rome and was appointed painter to the king. Illustrated an edition of Don Quijote. His brother, Isidro, was director of the Academy in Madrid.

JUAN CARRENO DE MIRANDA 1614-1685

Born in Avilés and studied in Madrid under Pedro de la Cuevas and Bartolomé Román. Was introduced to the Court by Velázquez. In 1671 became court painter to Charles II. He died in Madrid.

ANTONIO DEL CASTILLO SAAVEDRA 1616-1668

Born in Cordoba. His talent was so great that his works have often been compared to those of Zurbaran and even to those of Velazquez. He studied in Seville under Zurbaran, but later returned to Cordoba where he continued to work for the rest of his life. His salient qualities are a great firmness of drawing and a true freedom as to composition.

EUGENIO CAXES 1577-1642
Born in Madrid, a pupil of his father, Patricio, who was of Italian origin and brought to Spain by Philip II to collaborate in the decorations of El Escorial. Eugenio was educated in Spain and was thoroughly naturalized. He painted for the royal palaces; was a close friend of Carducho and often worked with him.

PABLO DE CESPEDES 1538-1608
Painter, sculptor and poet, born in Cordoba. He lived in Seville, where he became a collector of antiques and rare books. He travelled to Italy in several occasions, where he studied and worked in Rome. He died in his home town, yet his greatest production was executed in Seville.

CLAUDIO COELLO 1642-1693
Born in Madrid and a student of Francisco Rizi. He is considered the last worthy representative of the school of Madrid. He was active in Saragossa, and in 1685 became court painter to Charles II. He fully merited the high esteem in which he was held in his prime. It is true that he was greatly influenced by various styles of his time.

JUAN CONCHILLOS FALCO 1641-1711
Born in Valencia and considered an historical painter. Founded a school in his native city. Executed a number of altar pieces for churches in Murcia and Valencia. Became blind and paralyzed in his late years.

JERONIMO JACINTO ESPINOSA 1600-1667
Born in Concentaina and died in Valencia. He was a pupil of Francisco Ribalta who greatly influenced his work. He executed a large number of religious compositions for churches and monasteries in Valencia.

FRANCISCO DE GOYA Y LUCIENTES 1746-1828
Great man and painter of Spain. Born in the poor village of Fuendetodos, near Saragossa. Studied under Francisco Bayeu, whose daughter, Josefa, he married. Studied in Rome and Parma. A man of rare versatility, he was able to create with enormous power and incredible success in almost any medium. His satirical cartoons were serious political accusations of the time. There is no doubt that he was one of the most powerful artistic forces of his generation. His genius has not been surpassed to date by an artist of his country. He died in 1828 in Bordeaux.

EL GRECO 1541-1614

Domenico Theotocopulos, born in Crete and naturalized a Spaniard. A pupil of Titian, he was also influenced and guided by Tintoretto and Jacopo Bassano. He lived a secluded life in Toledo where he died, devoting himself greatly to religious painting.

JOSE GUTIERREZ DE LA VEGA 1832—

Painter of historic themes and portraits. Born in Seville and became Director of the Academy in that city. He exhibited a collection of his portraits in Paris, 1855.

FRANCISCO HERRERA THE YOUNG 1622-1685

Son and pupil of his father, Herrera el Viejo, (the Elder). This is one of the masters of the School of Seville. He broke away from his father and travelled to Italy, studying frescoes in Rome and thus acquired a sense of color. He was a clever interpreter of natural objects, fruit, game, fish. He followed the study of still life which he learned from his father.

FRANCISCO HERRERA THE ELDER 1576-1656

Born in Seville where he worked almost all of his life. The school of Seville owes him a new development and technique based on freedom and courage. He set before himself grandiose and magnificent ideals. Masses of light and color in audacious contrasts. He died in Madrid leaving a profound influence in the art of Spain.

SEBASTIAN HERRERA BARNUEVO 1619—

Born in Madrid. Was a painter, architect and sculptor like his father. He worked for many churches in the Spanish court site. Was greatly appreciated by the sovereigns and received several titles and appointments.

JUAN DE JUANES 1523-1579

Born Vicente Juanes, in Valencia. Studied in Rome and founded his style on the works of Raphael. He returned to Valencia where he gave great impetus to the art of his land.

FELIPE DE LIANO—d. 1625

Pupil of Alonso Sanchez Coello who showed great facility in the production of small oil portraits. Little is known of his life. He died in Madrid.

MARIANO MAELLA 1739-1819

Born in Valencia and studied in the Academy of San Fernando, Madrid. He worked for several years in Rome; upon his return to Spain he worked under the direction of Mengs. Was appointed court painter and director of the great academy, having Goya as sub-director. Considered one of the finest academic painters of his time.

17

BARTOLOME ESTEBAN MURILLO 1617-1682

Born in Seville of such humble origin that he studied with Juan del Castillo in the capacity of a servant. He was a friend of Velazquez, who helped lodge him in his brief stay at the court. He founded the Academy of Painting in Seville, where he worked mostly until his death.

JUAN FERNANDEZ NAVARRETE c.1526-1579

Born in Logrono and called "el Mudo" (the mute) he became deaf at the age of three and was unable to learn to speak. He studied in Italy and was influenced by Correggio and Titian. He was employed at the court and worked in El Escorial.

PEDRO ORRENTE c.1570-1645

Born in Murcia. He studied in Valencia, but worked mostly in Toledo with El Greco's son. Palomino asserts that he was an officer of the Inquisition. He died in Valencia.

FRANCISCO PACHECO 1564-1654

Born in Andalusia at San Lucar de Barrameda. He studied in Seville and visited Madrid and Toledo where he met el Greco. He formed a school in Seville. An eminent painter, he was also a literary figure of his time. He accompanied Velazquez to Madrid where he remained working for two years. Died in Seville.

BLAS DEL PARDO c.1545- c.1600

Born in Toledo where he worked and died. Little is known of his life.

LUIS PARET Y ALCAZAR 1747-1799

Painter, etcher and designer, born in Madrid. Obtained prizes at the Academy of San Fernando, of which he later became a member. Did a series of illustrations for Don Quijote. Died in Madrid.

ANTONIO PEREDA 1599-1678

Born in Valladolid, same year in which Velazquez was born in Seville. His style is peculiar and essentially Spanish. He belonged to a respectable family and was sent to study in Madrid while still very young. His work may possibly bear resemblance to the painting of Ribera.

FRANCISCO PRECIADO DE LA VEGA 1713-1789

A Sevillian who resided most of his life in Rome. He was appointed painter to the Camara of Ferdinand VI and director of the Spanish Academy in Rome.

FRANCISCO RIBALTA c.1551-1628

One of the first Spanish artists to use chiaroscuro in the manner of Caravaggio and his followers. His vigorous tonality and freedom of technique shows the influence of the school of Valencia, where he died.

JUSEPE RIBERA 1588-1652

Born near Valencia and studied with Ribalta. While still very young he went to Italy and settled in Naples. He was greatly favored by the intellectual classes. Called "lo Spagnoletto" he made much money and was treated kindly in Italy. His free and masterly technique place him amongst the great masters of all times. His output was vast and greatly influenced the painting of Spain.

JUAN VALDES DE LEAL 1630-1690

Born in Seville, and at one time rival of Velazquez. He spent his youth in Cordoba where he studied under Antonio del Castillo. Together with Murillo he formed the Academy of Painting at Seville, of which he was president. It is known that he worked in Madrid around 1764. He died in Seville.

LUIS DE VARGAS 1502-1568

Born in Seville; a pupil of Diego de la Barrera. He was greatly influenced by Roman mannerists, whose style he introduced to Seville.

DIEGO VELAZQUEZ 1599-1660

Studied under Herrera el Viejo and Francisco Pacheco, whose daughter he married. In 1622 was appointed court painter to Philip IV. Was in close contact with Rubens while the Flemish master visited Madrid. He had been influenced by Tintoretto and had visited Venice, Rome and Parma before 1631. Son of a noble family. His genius is revealed in a generous production, mostly executed in court, and his achievements are universally praised and admired as those of one of the greatest masters of all time.

FRANCISCO ZURBARAN 1598-1661

Born in Badajoz, but considered a Sevillian artist. Studied in Seville under Diaz de Villanueva and Roelas. He combined a great decorative talent with a vigorous execution. He loved to paint immovable figures engaged in meditation and repose. Velazquez admired him greatly and used his influence to have Philip IV appoint him as collaborator in the decorations of the Buen Retiro Palace.

PABLO de CESPEDES   Betrothal of St. Catherine

Jovellanos Collection, Gijón

22

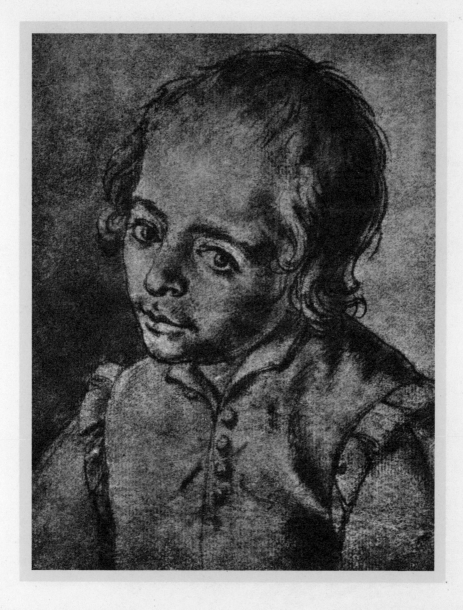

LUIS DE VARGAS   Portrait of a Boy

Kunsthalle, Hamburg

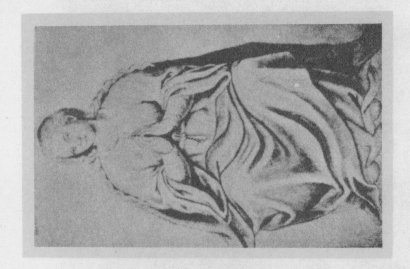

FRANCISCO PACHECO

St. John of Patmos

British Museum, London

JUAN DE JUANES

A Sketch for the Coronation of the Virgin

Prado Museum, Madrid

Dromedaries

Jovellanos Collection, Gijón

LUIS de VARGAS

BLAS del PARDO   Girl with Dove

Uffizi, Florence

26

NAVARRETE "EL MUDO"　　　　　　　　　　　Study of a Figure

British Museum, London

EL GRECO

National Library, Madrid

St. John The Evangelist

EL GRECO   St. Matthew (detail)

Farquhar Oliver Collection, London

29

FRANCISCO RIBALTA ——————————————— St. Bruno (detail)

St. Carlos Academy, Valencia

30

JUSEPE DE RIBERA   Old Woman

Christ Church Collection, Oxford

HERRERA, THE ELDER   The Apostle of St. Thomas
                    British Museum, London

FRANCISCO PACHECO   Studies of the Nude

Albertina, Vienna

33

EUGENIO CAXES
Miracle of St. Bruno

Albertina, Vienna

PEDRO ORRENTE   Man Seated

St. Carlos Academy, Valencia

35

JUSEPE DE RIBERA   Aparition of the Child

Royal Print Cabinet, Munich

36

FRANCISCO ZUBARAN   St. Hieronymus

Louvre Museum, Paris

VELAZQUEZ   Head of a Girl

National Library, Madrid

JUSEPE DE RIBERA   Saint, (detail of Aparition of the Child)
                          Royal Print Cabinet, Munich

HERRERA THE ELDER   A Sketch

Uffizi, Florence

VELAZQUEZ

National Library, Madrid

Male Head

VELAZQUEZ

British Museum, London

Studies of Horses

42

VELAZQUEZ   Portrait of a Boy

Royal Print Cabinet, Munich

43

ANTONIO PEREDA

Jovellanos Collection, Gijón

Study of Heads

HERRERA THE ELDER   A Sketch

Uffizi, Florence

JUSEPE DE RIBERA

Man Chastised by Cupid

Condé Museum, Chantilly

46

JUSEPE DE RIBERA   *Albertina, Vienna*   The Crucifixion of St. Peter

VELAZQUEZ

British Museum, London

Portrait of a Child

JUSEPE DE RIBERA   The Artist's Daughter

Filangeri Museum, Naples

JACINTO ESPINOSA   Christ Bearing the Cross

St. Carlos Academy, Valencia

VELAZQUEZ

British Museum, London

Bishop on Horseback

51

FRANCISCO ZURBARAN   Monk

British Museum, London

VELAZQUEZ   Cardinal Borja

St. Fernando Academy, Madrid

ALONSO CANO   Loves

Condé Museum, Chantilly

54

ALONSO CANO   Angels Ministering to St. Sebastian
Metropolitan Museum of Art, New York

MURILLO   *British Museum, London*   Sketch for St. Isidore

CARRENO DE MIRANDA   The Miracle of St. Isidore
                Academy of San Fernando, Madrid

DEL CASTILLO Y SAAVEDRA   Raising of the Cross (detail)
Uffizi, Florence

DEL CASTILLO SAAVEDRA   Martyrdom of St. Catherine
                    Uffizi, Florence

Design for an Altar

Louvre Museum, Paris

ALONSO CANO

Kunsthalle, Hamburg

MURILLO

MURILLO   Ascension of the Virgin

Kunsthalle, Hamburg

62

MURILLO

Louvre Museum, Paris

St. Anthony of Padua

MURILLO   Adoration of the Virgin and Child
                        Condé Museum, Chantilly

64

MURILLO   Angels (detail from St. Anthony of Padua)
                    Louvre Museum, Paris

MURILLO   St. Joseph and the Infant Jesus

Louvre Museum, Paris

MURILLO

The Pierpont Morgan Library, New York

St. Felix of Cantalicio

67

SEBASTIAN DE HERRERA BARNUEVO
National Library, Madrid

Sketch for Jael de Sisera

MURILLO

Betrothal of St. Catherine

Kunsthalle, Hamburg

HERRERA "EL MOZO"   Resurrection of Christ

National Library, Madrid

FELIPE de LIANO   The Virgin with the Child Jesus

Albertina, Vienna

CLAUDIO COELLO   Sketch of a Portrait

Uffizi, Florence

72

CLAUDIO COELLO   Portrait

Louvre Museum, Paris

JOSE ANTOLINEZ   Sketch for The Immaculate Conception
                 The Hispanic Society of America

74

CAMARON y BORONAT   St. John the Baptist

The Hispanic Society of America

MARIANO MAELLA   *The Hispanic Society of America*   St. Benedict

JUAN DE VALDES LEAL   Head of St. John the Baptist

Kunsthalle, Hamburg

MARIANO MAELLA   The Last Supper

National Library, Madrid

RAMON BAYEU Y SUBIAS   Sheet of Studies with Five Figures
National Library, Madrid

CONCHILLOS y FALCO   The Baptism of Christ (detail)
The Hispanic Society of America

FRANCISCO BAYEU Y SUBIAS

National Library, Madrid

The Picnic

ANTONIO CARNICERO   Ascent of the Montgolfier Balloon

Kunsthalle, Hamburg.

CAMARON Y BORONAT   Spanish Women
            National Library, Madrid

GOYA   The Garter

Prado Museum, Madrid

GOYA

Prado Museum, Madrid

"Horrible to look at"

GOYA   Study

British Museum, London

86

GOYA   Portrait of the Duke of Wellington

British Museum, London

GOYA   Duchess of Alba with negrita María de la Luz
                        Prado Museum, Madrid

GOYA   Awaiting

Prado Museum, Madrid

GOYA   Procession

Prado Museum, Madrid

90

GOYA "Less savage than others"

Prado Museum, Madrid

PRECIADO DE LA VEGA   Design for a Fan
The Hispanic Society of America

"Don't open your eyes"

Prado Museum, Madrid

GOYA

GOYA

The Frick Collection, New York

Anglers under a Rock

GOYA   Construction in Progress

Metropolitan Museum of Art, New York

GOYA   Sedan-chairman

Gerstenberg Collection, Berlin

GOYA   The Garrote

British Museum, London

98

GOYA   Andalusian Dance

Prado Museum, Madrid

GUTIERREZ DE LA VEGA

National Library, Madrid

Andalusian Dance